# Looking at Small Mammals

# Small Cats

## Sally Morgan

### Chrysalis Children's Books

First published in the UK in 2004 by
Chrysalis Children's Books
An imprint of Chrysalis Books Group Plc
The Chrysalis Building, Bramley Road
London W10 6SP

Editorial manager: Joyce Bentley
Series editor: Debbie Foy
Editors: Clare Lewis, Joseph Fullman
Designer: Wladek Szechter
Picture researcher: Sally Morgan
Illustrations: Woody

ISBN 1 84458 104 7

Printed in China

10 9 8 7 6 5 4 3 2 1

British Library Cataloguing in Publication Data for this
book is available from the British Library.

Picture acknowledgements:
Ecoscene: 3B, 6, 9, 21B, 32 Peter Cairns; 19T Brian
Cushing; 5B, 26 Robert Gill; 15T Michael Maconachie;
12B, 17 Jack Milchanowski; 1, 2, 4, 5T, 7T & 7B, 8,
10, 11T & 11B, 15B, 16, 18, 19B, 20, 21T, 22, 23, 25T,
25B Robert Pickett; 9T, 24 John Pitcher; 27B Fritz
Polking; 14 Gehan de Silva, 27T Satyendra Tiwari.
Front cover: TL Jack Milchanowski; B, TCL, TCR,
TR, CL & CR Robert Pickett. Back cover: TL Jack
Milchanowski; TCL, TCR, TR Robert Pickett. Frank
Lane Picture Agency: 13T Silvestris. Getty Images: 3T
Photodisc Blue. Still Pictures: 13B Martin Harvey.

# Contents

# What are small cats?

The small cats belong to a group of animals called **mammals**. Most mammals have four legs and are covered in hair. They give birth to live young.

*The lynx is covered in thick fur.*

4

*The wild cat could be mistaken for a pet cat.*

Young mammals feed on their mother's milk for the first months of their lives. The pet cat is an example of a small cat. Other small cats include bobcats, ocelots and lynxes. Cats are related to dogs, bears and weasels.

*The puma or cougar is the largest of the small cats.*

5

# The cat family

The cat has a long, slender body and is covered in soft fur. Most cats have golden brown fur, but it may be patterned with circles, stripes or spots. In total, there are 28 different types of small cat.

*The grey-white fur of the lynx blends in with the snowy woodlands in which it lives.*

*The ocelot has a rounded head and a short muzzle. It has short, velvety fur.*

Cats are meat eaters or **carnivores**.

This means that they hunt other animals

and kill them

for food.

*Cats, such as this ocelot, have excellent senses to help them hunt.*

# Where do small cats live?

Small cats are found all over the world, except in Australia, New Zealand and Antarctica.

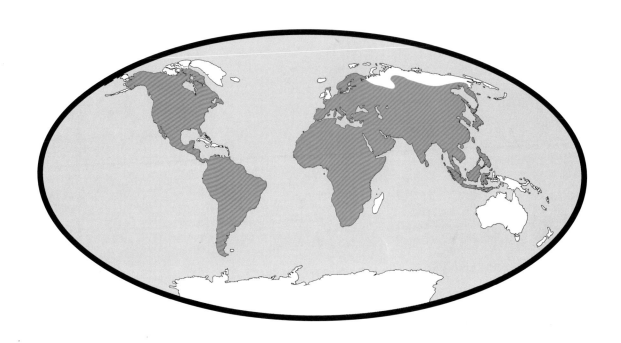

*The areas shaded in pink on this map of the world show where small cats live.*

*The puma is found across North America. This puma is hunting along a river.*

They live in

many different

types of habitat.

They are found in tropical rainforests, in

cold northern forests, on grassland and

even in deserts.

*The European lynx is found in cold northern forests where snow lies on the ground for many months.*

# What do cats eat?

Small cats prey on, or hunt, smaller animals. Their **prey** ranges in size from small frogs and fish, to lizards and large birds.

*This young bobcat has caught a mouse.*

*This puma has killed a deer by a river.*

Some eat small mammals such as rats and mice. The cougar hunts large mammals such as mule deer and elk.

*Lynxes feed on birds and small mammals.*

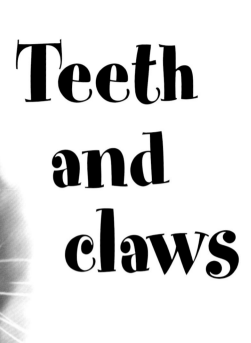

# Teeth and claws

Cats have sharp teeth and claws to catch, grip and kill their prey. They have four large pointed teeth at the front of their mouth called **canines**.

*A snarling bobcat shows its long canine teeth.*

*This lynx has tracked down its prey and is using its strong teeth to tear flesh.*

These teeth are for stabbing and gripping their prey. They have large teeth at the back of their mouths to slice off bits of meat and to crush bone.

*Sharp claws are used to grip the prey.*

# Hunting for food

Cats use their senses to find their prey.

Many cats hunt at dawn and dusk when there is less light. During the day cats can see as well as people.

*A serval creeps up on its prey using its eyes and ears.*

14

*The two forward-facing eyes of a cat allow it to judge distances very well.*

They also have excellent night vision and can see a lot of detail in the dark.

They use their other senses at night too.

Cats have large ears to trap sounds and a good sense of smell to find prey.

*Cats have long hairs called **whiskers** around their mouths, which are very sensitive. They help the cat to feel its way at night.*

# Getting around

Small cats can move quickly over the ground.

They are **sprinters**, which means that they can

run fast over a short distance.

*A cat can jump distances
many times the length of
its own body.*

*A lynx climbs up a rocky slope looking for prey.*

They have to run fast to catch prey such as hares and deer. Most small cats can climb trees too. They use their sharp claws to grip the tree to climb. Their eyes can judge distances when they jump from branch to branch. When cats fall, they twist in the air so that they land on their feet.

# Spotted coats

Many small cats have spotted or striped coats. This helps them to blend in with their background so they cannot be seen easily. This is called **camouflage**.

*This ocelot is difficult to spot as it lies in the **undergrowth**.*

*Ocelots have pale coats with both spots and stripes.*

In a forest, the light comes through the trees forming shadows on the ground.

A cat that has brown fur with darker stripes or spots is well hidden in the shadows.

*The serval has a golden brown coat with darker stripes, dashes and spots.*

# Talking to each other

Big cats such as the lion and tiger roar. Small cats cannot roar, but they can purr.

*The raised tail of this pet cat tell us that it is happy.*

*An angry wild cat flattens its ears.*

Cats purr when they are happy. They growl or hiss when they are angry. Cats use their tails to communicate too. An angry cat swishes its tail from side to side while a happy cat lifts its tail up.

*Lynxes rub their heads against each other when they meet as a greeting.*

# Cats and their kittens

When it is time to have her kittens, a female cat finds a safe place to build her nest. It may be in a **burrow** or cave, or under a fallen tree.

*One-week-old kittens feed on their mother's milk.*

*Young kittens spend much of their time asleep.*

A female cat gives birth to between one and four tiny babies called kittens. The kittens are born with their eyes closed so they are blind. They are covered in fur.

# Looking after their young

The kittens stay in their nest for a few weeks. It is safe in the nest. They feed on their mother's milk.

*A young puma explores its surroundings.*

24

*This bobcat kitten is fed and cleaned by its mother.*

When they get older they go outside to play. Soon they follow their mother and learn how to hunt. They stay close to their mother for many months until they are fully grown and can look after themselves.

*This lynx kitten is just seven weeks old.*

# Big relatives

Small cats have some well-known big relatives. These are the lion, tiger, cheetah, leopard and jaguar. The tiger is the largest of the big cats and lives alone in the forests of India and south-east Asia.

*The lion lives in a group called a pride.*

26

*The Bengal tiger lives in the forests of India.*

The lion lives on grasslands in Africa. The cheetah lives in Africa too. It is the fastest of all land animals

*The cheetah creeps up close on its prey and then gives chase.*

# Investigate!

## Watching pet cats

Many people have a pet cat. Watch a cat to see how it behaves. Look at how the tail moves when it is happy or angry. Listen to the sounds it makes when it is happy. Find out how it sharpens its claws. Follow a cat into the garden and watch how it hunts.

*Cats like to sharpen their claws on tree trunks or other rough surfaces.*

*Watch what happens to a cat's fur when it is angry, but take care!*

# Paw prints

When snow covers the ground, go outside and look for the tracks of cats and dogs. Can you see any differences between the paw print of a cat and a dog? Count the number of toes. Can you see the claw marks on the cat print? How far apart are the individual paw prints?

*Look out for cats' footprints in your garden. How many toes can you count on each paw?*

# Visiting zoos

Many small cats, such as ocelots and lynxes are kept in zoos and wildlife centres where you can see them in natural-looking surroundings. You can watch them move and eat. You can also find out more about small cats by reading books and searching on the Internet.

# Cat facts

✓ The bobcat is named after its short tail.

✓ The serval leaps more than a metre into the air to pounce on its prey.

✓ The fishing cat dives into water to catch fish or waterbirds.

✓ The margay is an excellent climber and is able to run down a tree trunk head first or hang from a branch with one paw.

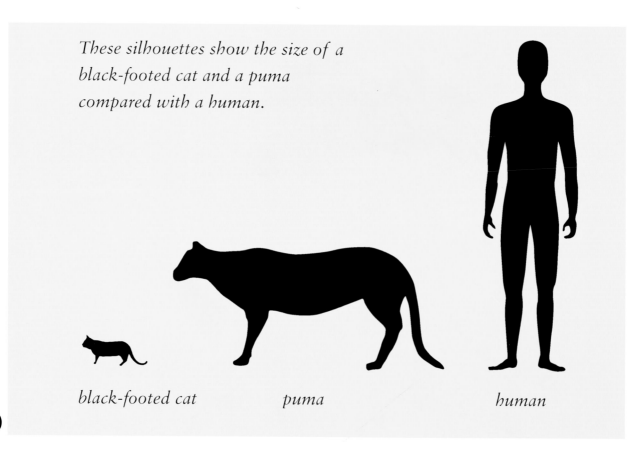

*These silhouettes show the size of a black-footed cat and a puma compared with a human.*

*black-footed cat*   *puma*   *human*

# Glossary

**burrow** a large hole or tunnel in the ground.

**camouflage** colours that blend in with the background to make it very difficult to see an animal.

**canine** a large pointed tooth near the front of the cat's mouth which is used to stab and grip prey.

**carnivore** an animal that eats other animals.

**mammal** an animal that feeds their young with milk and is covered in fur.

**prey** an animal that is hunted by other animals.

**sprinter** a person or animal that can run very fast over a short distance.

**undergrowth** low growing plants on the ground, usually under trees.

**whisker** stiff hair found around the mouth and nose of a mammal.

# Index